Breaking
the Silence

Breaking
the Silence

A Story of Redemption from the Trauma of Abortion

Anita Grace Gaddis

authorHOUSE®

AuthorHouse™
1663 Liberty Drive
Bloomington, IN 47403
www.authorhouse.com
Phone: 1-800-839-8640

Published by AuthorHouse 10/24/2014

ISBN: 978-1-4918-2957-8 (sc)
ISBN: 978-1-4918-2956-1 (e)

Library of Congress Control Number: 2013923515

Contents

Acknowledgments..ix

Introduction..xi

Little Girl Loved...1

It Seemed Good to Me Also 2

Demons 4

Guilt 5

Post-Abortion Syndrome..8

I Can Do It by Myself 10

Spring Revival, 2011 12

Grace, Grace, and More Grace!.................................14

Survival Mode..16

Pain..19

September 11, 2001 Paints a Picture 22

Ashes..24

Mother's Day..26

Baby Girl or Baby Boy?..29

The Book of Esther 30

Surrendering the Secret..33

Comfort...35

Refuge Crisis Pregnancy Center................................37

Lexigrace...39

December 30, 2011...44

A Final Note 45

Bibliography...47

First and foremost, I dedicate this book to my husband, Keith. He has stood by me for many years, knowing I was suffering from post-traumatic stress from an abortion in 1984, and praying for God to heal me. I would not be where I am today without his continuous mental, physical, and spiritual support in my life. I thank God for bringing us together in 1985 and keeping us together for all these years.

Second, I dedicate this book to my three living children, April, Shelby, and Luke, who unbeknownst to them, God used greatly as a balm for my heartsick soul. Over the years, they have sacrificed much by being my children. I thank God for them, and I pray He will richly reward them for their patience with me during the homeschooling years!

Within the echo of their innocent laughter, I could hear a tiny voice from the edges of heaven whispering, "Mama." A voice that cried out to be heard just like theirs—the voice of my Lexigrace—the baby I loved too late.

The Spirit of the Lord God is upon me, because the Lord has anointed me to bring good news to the suffering and afflicted. He has sent me to comfort the broken-hearted, to announce liberty to the captives and to open the eyes of the blind. He has sent me to tell those who mourn that the time of God's favor to them has come, and the day of his wrath to their enemies. To all who mourn in Israel He will give: Beauty for ashes; Joy instead of mourning; Praise instead of heaviness. For God has planted them like strong and graceful oaks for His own glory. And they shall rebuild the ancient ruins, repairing cities long ago destroyed; reviving them though they have lain there many generations.

—Isaiah 61:1-4 (TLB)

Acknowledgments

Where would I be today without the love of my Lord Jesus Christ? He is the one who inspired me to write from the overflow of the thanksgiving in my heart. I am so grateful that He let me live long enough to come to a place of healing. Thank you, Lord!

Keith, thank you for staying with me through the good and the bad days. Your commitment to our marriage is to be praised because I was so hard to live with some days. I wish that I could have been the bride you deserved from the start. Thank you for your love and gentleness. You are the kindest person I know.

April, my sweet baby girl, little did you know how God was using you through the years to restore me. You were my first living child. What a privilege it has been to be your mama! I cannot express my joy about what you are doing with your life as a nurse. If not for that day that I spent with you when you volunteered at the pregnancy center, I might not have walked this road to recovering from the post-traumatic stress of an abortion. Maybe one day God will put us back in the same state, and we can open our own crisis pregnancy center!

Shelby, my precious, darling girl, you have no idea what a gift you are from God to me. Even as a child, you have been a source of comfort for me. You've held my hand

and wiped my tears without asking questions. I will never forget the day you gently said, "Its okay, Mom. Whatever you've done—it's okay." I have never felt more loved. You gave me acceptance long before you ever knew the story behind my pain and tears. Thank you for loving me.

Luke, my son, my happy-go-lucky boy, who makes me laugh out loud. I couldn't have lived life without you! You've had a special place in my heart right from the start. Even though I made lots of mistakes while you lived at home with us, I see no judgement in your beautiful brown eyes. That speaks volumes to me because I don't deserve the love that you give unconditionally. I messed up, Luke. Pure and simple, but God blessed me with you, and I am forever grateful.

I would especially like to acknowledge Cindy Howard, Joni Perry, and Mrs. Cherie Mullins. Your walk with the Lord has been my inspiration for many years. You have ministered to my heart through your gift of singing. You carry yourselves with grace, and you have extended mercy to this broken-hearted, sometimes undeserving girl. You have laughed with me and cried with me. Thank you.

To the ladies at Glen Haven Baptist church, you are so special to me because you didn't turn away when I shared my story with you. Your hugs comforted me and helped me make it through another day. You listened to me without making judgements. You cheered me on with many words of encouragement. Your friendship is priceless!

Introduction

Why would I want to write that I had an abortion in 1984, just thirteen days before my twenty-first birthday?

Honestly, twenty-nine years ago, I would never have dreamed of writing about this, mainly because the one time I told someone, that person assured me that I was cursed and sent me literature and a little clay angel figurine to "guard over me." So for many years afterward, I lived with the fear that I was cursed forever. I remember being so haunted by it all that, one day, I took the clay angel figurine outside and smashed it into a million pieces with a hammer! I guess I thought the fear of being cursed would go away if I didn't have to look at that guardian angel every day, but the truth was still the horrible truth; I'd had an abortion.

I know that sharing my story today is not going to fix that. It will never be fixed this side of heaven, but after wrestling it out with God, I have realized that I must put this down on paper as a testimony to His awesome mercy and grace—especially His grace.

In 2011, God tenderly brought healing in my heart, one day at a time. It was then, for the first time ever, that I was able to grieve over my loss. Ever since that moment, I have started to take back the years that were spent in silence about the effects of abortion. I have a passion to help abortion-minded people and post-abortive women. He has "led me beside the still waters and he has restored my soul" Psalm 23:2 (NKJV).

As for being cursed, I know that, with God, all things are possible. He can break the curse that I brought on by having an abortion, so I cling to the scriptures that Joel penned in Joel 2:13. "Return to the Lord your God, for He is gracious and compassionate, slow to anger and abounding in love, and <u>He relents from sending calamity.</u>" Another verse that I can't live without is found in Galatians 3:1314. "Christ redeemed us from the curse of the law by becoming a curse for us . . . so that by faith we might receive the promise of the Spirit."

One of my favorite bible study leaders is Beth Moore. I learned in her study on *James; Mercy Triumphs* that God can change everything about a curse. God can take a curse off of me forever! What wonderful news!! Wow! Could it be that in the healing process, as I began to use my pain to help others, God miraculously turned my sordid past that could have been a curse into a gift? As I look back over the years, I see His hand guiding me through troubled waters and bringing me through them to a place where my story can be used for His glory.

He can truly bring beauty from ashes, can't He?

Little Girl Loved

"Come with me little girl," I heard my Father say.
"We're gonna climb a mountain, and we need to start today.
This valley that you're living in, I'm filling up with dirt.
I've bottled up your tears and loved away the hurt."

"I love you, little girl," I heard my Father say.
"The path is steep and rocky, but I'm with you all the way.
There's sunshine on the mountaintop and
Flowers for you to see, and as you
You slowly climb along, I'll keep you company."

Love, Jesus

It Seemed Good to Me Also

As I began to heal from the trauma of an abortion, I felt compelled to write. The enemy, Satan, started whispering lies about how writing would be stupid and nobody would ever read it. After attending a Beth Moore simulcast in 2011, I felt reassured by God's word that I needed to write.

> In as much as many have taken in hand to set in order a narrative of those things which have been fulfilled among us, just as those who from the beginning were eyewitnesses and ministers of the word delivered them to us, it seemed good to me also, having had a perfect understanding of all things from the very first, to write to you an orderly account. (Luke 1:13) NKJV

Yes, there is plenty of material out now for post-abortive women and men that is very helpful, but just like Luke, I felt I needed to write my account because "it seemed good to me also." This is for my family. This is for my friends. This is for anyone who has had an abortion—a person who wants to be healed but is afraid of all that he or she must go through to get the heart to a healing place.

I write this for my heavenly Father, who has brought me to this season in life and kept me safe. From the minute I walked out of the doors of the abortion clinic, my Savior began to set in motion a plan of redemption. He chose a path that would lead me to my husband, Keith, and on to the church that I am a member of today. Glen Haven Baptist Church is a haven, a resting place for me to grow spiritually and learn that God is not just encouraging us to follow the rules, but He is a good God who restores broken people.

Most of all, this is for my grandchildren and great-grandchildren who have yet to be born. I want them to know that abortion should never be an option, no matter what their circumstances are. I want to leave my family with an understanding about the trauma of abortion so that the generations to come will have the chance to live and praise the Lord. One thing I have learned after many years of suffering heartache and grief in silence is that I do not want my children or grandchildren to become post-abortive. It would break my heart!

"This will be written for the generation to come, so that a people yet to be created may praise the Lord!" (Psalm 102:18).

Demons

Plagued by a hundred demons,
She knew the reason why.
And when they all came calling,
She often thought she'd die.

At times the torture was so strong;
It was more than she could bear,
But she learned to run to Jesus
And cast on Him her care.

He would send the demons flying
And hide her 'neath His wing.
Her prince
      Her shield
      Her defender—Her Majesty, the King.

Guilt

After Keith and I were married we attended church sporadically. When April, our oldest daughter, was born, we knew she needed to be in Sunday school. We began to make the effort to go to church every Sunday morning. By the time our third child, Luke, was born, we went regularly. I began to work hard at concealing the fact that I'd had an abortion. I was tormented by guilt while I was faithfully attending church. I was desperate for help, but I still didn't want to share my story for many reasons—the biggest was for fear of embarrassing Keith. By this time in our lives, we had become very involved in different ministries at church. What would people think of his choice for a wife?

I had grown up in a Christian home and had learned at an early age that God frowns on sin. What I didn't learn was that He is a loving God who stands ready to forgive us when we fail Him. After my abortion, I was filled with guilt and shame for what I had done.

In a program called H.E.A.R.T., I learned about true guilt. True guilt brings about conviction of sinful behavior, which leads to confession of sin and repentance. God tells us that when we ask for forgiveness, He will forgive us.

Then there is false guilt. H.E.A.R.T. says it is a "direct attack from the enemy", Satan. He uses false guilt to keep us in bondage. Satan is smart. He knows that a forgiven child of God is able to reveal his plan so he works constantly to keep us in a prison of false guilt.

I suffered with false guilt for many years. I asked God to forgive me over and over for my sin of abortion, but I didn't get victory from the guilt. I wanted to be free of it, but I didn't understand how I could overcome it. I thought I should beat myself up daily for what I had done. Living this way took a toll on me physically at times because I used food as a punishment for my past mistake. I would either withhold it altogether or I would eat and then make myself throw it back up. I know that, for several years, I was bordering on being bulimic.

Just like there is true guilt and false guilt, H.E.A.R.T. describes healthy shame and unhealthy shame. Guess which one I lived with? Yes, I was a star pupil in the unhealthy shame category!

Healthy shame is good. It uses our conscience to help us be holy. Unhealthy shame, on the other hand, is not about what we did but about who we think we are. It is based on our feelings of self-worth. It makes us feel like we will be rejected if people know the truth about us. My unhealthy shame kept me from enjoying life. From my emotions to my marriage, I needed to be in control of everything. I was afraid to let my husband make the decisions and be the spiritual leader in our family. My little family suffered greatly because of the unhealthy shame that kept me in bondage.

In 2002, when the guilt and shame began to surface on a daily basis, I cautiously looked for help. By this time, I had heard enough, through Bible study and Sunday morning sermons, to know that I needed to deal with the root of my problem. I called a pregnancy resource center to inquire about post abortion counseling, but when the lady asked for my name, I hung up. I wanted help, but I wasn't ready to give my name to anyone who might know someone who knew me. Since it was still a big secret that I was ashamed, I wasn't about to go to Lifeway and ask for a book on post-abortion trauma. Finally, I called Focus on the Family, and they mailed me several books on the subject, including the following:

I Will Hold You in Heaven by Jack Hayford
Her Choice to Heal by Sydna Masse and Joan Philips

I am so thankful for those books! I found out that I was suffering from post-abortion syndrome. I realized, through reading Sydna's and Joan's testimonies, that what I was going through was normal after having an abortion. For a little while, I had relief from the guilt. I used the books as a bandaids for my hurting heart. I read them and then hid them in a bottom drawer. Occasionally, I took them out and used them to help me get through another year, another day another minute. God used the information in these books to keep me pressing on until I got to a place where I was ready to get counseling.

Post-Abortion Syndrome

Having an abortion left a hole in my heart. I was filled with regret and anger. As I mentioned earlier, I used food to punish myself. I often thought of committing suicide. My procedure was done on May 9 which is close to Mother's Day, so I always had an increased anxiety level around my anniversary date. In H.E.A.R.T., I learned that post-abortion syndrome carried the acronym PAS, and its symptoms can bring about a type of post-traumatic stress disorder. Some women may have a delayed reaction long after having an abortion, but I was affected continuously.

For example, I was terrified of going to the dentist. I even went for several years without dental care. When I finally had to take care of urgent dental problems, my husband went with me and held my hand as tears ran down my cheeks. He had to go with me several times before I could go by myself, and I was thirty years old! I know he and the dentist were bewildered about this because there was no explanation. I thought maybe I was afraid of the dentist because of an experience that I'd had as a very young child, but that didn't really make sense because I never had a problem during my teen years.

Then when I began seeking healing from my abortion, I read that the tools in a dental office sound a lot like the tools used in an abortion clinic. Suddenly it made perfect sense as to why I was so scared of the dentist. The sounds from that day were stored away in my subconscience. Amazing! I finally had an answer to my fears of the dentist. Armed with this knowledge, I began to ask God to help me heal so I could go to the dentist by myself.

Startling easily was another way PAS effected me. There were times when Keith walked into a room and startled me so badly that I jumped out of my skin! I yelled at him for scaring me, and then he got so aggravated at me because he didn't think I should be afraid of him walking into the room. Keith was right, but I wasn't like other people; I wasn't normal.

We didn't understand or connect my startling to the abortion until I went through counseling. I found out that being jumpy can be a symptom of being traumatized from the abortion.

I had eating disorders, survival guilt, anniversary syndrome, and thoughts of suicide. I went through life feeling numb most of the time. I worked hard at keeping the anxiety, anger, grief, and guilt buried deep inside of me. It took a lot of energy. Some days the stress of the present along with the stress of the past was just too much to deal with, and I would just lose it. My husband caught the brunt of it. That he has stayed by my side for all this time is a miracle. An absolute miracle.

I Can Do It by Myself

I really believed that I could handle the symptoms of PAS all by myself. Most of my symptoms were under control for the most part. My extended family and church friends didn't know, and I thought that I would be okay if I told God I was sorry every now and then.

I also thought if I pulled out one of the books I had ordered previously and read through it again, I would make it out of the depression that threatened to take me under. As long as I doctored the old wounds, I thought I was healing. My spiritual infection ran deep though, and after a while, little by little, the old feelings started coming back—the doubts, the fear of being cursed, the pain from the memory of that day, the uncertainty of not knowing if I would go to heaven or not, the thoughts of suicide. These thoughts began to torment me; I knew I needed professional help.

Keith urged me to seek Christian counseling from a lady in my church, Dr. Coralie Cox, lovingly known as Mrs. Kitty. I met with her on Monday afternoons and was given the assurance that God loved me no matter what I had done. Her acceptance and belief in me went a long way toward getting me to the next steps in the healing process. I began to realize that I was putting my abortion above the cross. I had held on to it for so long that it had become an idol. Wow! I had never thought of it like that before! If it was above the cross, then what was I saying to God? I was telling Him that His Son was not powerful enough to take this sin away from me! I believe I truly began to heal when I put my abortion back where it belonged—at the foot of the cross.

Spring Revival, 2011

In a 2011 spring revival at my church, Glen Haven Baptist, I heard an awesome speaker by the name of Chris Shepherd. He said, "God can't heal it unless I reveal it." The enemy, Satan, wants us to live in defeat, and he will do all that he can to keep us in bondage. He kept me there for many years, but I now have this verse in my arsenal "You intended to harm me, but God intended it for good" (Genesis 50:20). It was at this point that a light bulb went off in my head. I knew I needed to share my secret with my pastor and his wife. He was, after all, my spiritual leader of nineteen years. It was a big deal for me to go to him and tell him my story. It was also liberating. God was in the business of restoring my soul. All through 2011, He led me to different resources to find healing, real healing, the kind of healing that prompted me to reach out to others with my story.

It has taken many years, but today I know that I am forgiven. I am restored, and I am ready to share the events that led up to the day I walked into an abortion clinic. I know that God will never waste my pain. I've also come to the conclusion that if I don't confront the lies that abortion doesn't cause pain or regret, I am letting those who advocate it win. I don't want them to win.

Abortion is wrong on all kinds of levels. It destroys not only the physical life of your child, but also it destroys you. Please know that it doesn't solve your problem. It creates new problems. Please don't ever consider it an option. Across the country today, there are crisis pregnancy centers available to reach out to you and help you through an unplanned pregnancy. There are also post-abortive counselors available to help you heal from the trauma of abortion. Ask God to lead you to the right one for you. Trust me, He will.

Grace, Grace, and More Grace!

I was born into this world on May 22, 1963, and given the name Anita Grace. Unknowingly, my parents picked the perfect name for me. Anita is a derivative of Ann, which also means grace. I didn't like my name while growing up because it was not a common name or pretty to me. However, in time my name has become a blessing because I smile when I picture my heavenly Father looking down on me and shaking His head. He knew this girl was going to need an extra dose of grace—His grace—to get through life. The cool thing about my name is also in the numbers. Both Anita and Grace have five letters, and if you study numbers then you know that five is the number of grace! I imagine God saying, "Grace, grace, and more grace"!

I asked Christ into my heart when I was around seven years old. I loved Jesus so much at that age. I wanted to serve God so much that I told Him I was even willing to be a missionary!

So what happened to me? How did I get off track and get so far from God that I would commit such an atrocious sin? Honestly, I don't know. It's not like I got up one day and said, "I hate you God."

I was raised in some really legalistic, independent, Baptist churches. In seventh grade, I was placed in a Christian school. By my teens, God had become rules and judgement—no room for mercy or grace. Unconditional love was unthinkable. I remember, in my teens, at night, I crawled to the window in my room by my bed and looked up into the night sky. I cried out for God to forgive me, to hear me, to show me He still loved me. In my anger at my spiritual leaders, my heart grew very hard. Later on in my life, God brought me to Glen Haven Baptist Church in Decatur, Georgia. My pastor emeritus, Brother Ralph Easterwood, told us often that "rules without relationship bring rebellion." How true! I simply rebelled against the rules. In my rebellion, I slipped further and further from my precious, heavenly Father. I got so far away that I couldn't even hear His voice on that fateful day in 1984 at the abortion clinic. All I could think about was my own survival.

Survival Mode

Have you ever read this verse in the Bible? "Tender hearted women have cooked and eaten their own children; thus they survived the siege" (Lamentations 4:10 TLB).

Another version puts it this way. "With their own hands compassionate women have cooked their own children, who became their food when my people were destroyed" (Lamentations 4:10 NIV).

I know you are going to run and get a Bible and look it up. Go ahead. It's there. It is shocking to read and even harder to imagine, but life is hard and we make irreversible choices sometimes.

I'm sure none of the mothers described in that verse ever dreamed their children's lives would end like that, at their mothers' hands. It was such a terrible time that they could think only of their survival, and having to survive, whether physically or mentally, is a terrible position to be put in. Very rarely will human nature allow a person to choose another's survival over his or her own.

I was in survival mode that May day. I had already left home, and I couldn't bear to tell my parents. My mom has always been in bad health, and she and my dad had enough problems of their own. My relationship with them at the time was very strained, and I didn't want to risk further rejection.

To give a little background about my mom—when I was around eight years old, my mom became severely crippled with rheumatoid arthritis. She was in terrible pain. When I was twelve, she gave birth to my youngest sister, and immediately afterward, she had a nervous breakdown. She was so sick that my grandmother came to our house each day to help us. My dad was self-employed and worked hard to pay the bills. Many responsibilities were placed on my young shoulders; I had to become a caregiver at an early age. By the time I was eighteen, I was angry and tired. I wanted a life with no responsibilities, so I left home. I worked two jobs just so I could be independent and free.

Overnight, I went from having lots of rules to no rules at all. I began to party. Weekends were a blur. At the age of twenty-one, I found out I was pregnant, and I was devastated. What would I do? My independence would be over. The one person I confided in at the time told me that abortion was my only option. I knew the demands of taking care of a baby; after all, I had helped take care of my little sister for six years before leaving home. Sadly, human nature won over Christian principals in my life. I found a clinic listed in the yellow pages and made the appointment.

Outside it was a warm, beautiful day in May, but inside it was lonely, cold, and depressing. I paid my fee, put on a flimsy hospital gown, and waited my turn in a room full of girls dressed just like me. Finally, my name was called to go to the next room. Since I paid for anaesthesia, the last thing I remember was lying on a table with tears running down my cheeks and a nurse asking me if I was scared. Yes, I was scared! She told me it would soon be over.

In the recovery room, all I could think about was that I needed to get up and out of that building as fast as possible. I told the nurse that someone was with me when, in fact, that person had dropped me off. I ran downstairs and waited for a long time for my ride to pick me up. I can tell you, from that day on, I began to feel myself go numb. Emotionally, I started a withdrawal process that lasted for years.

It's only by the grace of God that I am still here today to tell you that there is mercy and peace in His arms. God is the only one who can make this right. Not me. Not you. Only God.

That's the hope I stand on today. In my life, one day at a time, God is making this terrible choice that I made right. I have been redeemed; I have been restored, and I want to tell of God's righteousness and love to anyone who has had an abortion. He forgave *me*, and I know that He will forgive you.

Pain

Here comes the pain, screaming again, dragging me back to where I've been.

Pulling me down and sucking me in, holding me tight like a long lost friend.

Just when I think I've put it behind, it sneaks across the thoughts in my mind.

Then it pokes and stabs like never before,

'Cause pain is greedy and always wants more.

What can I do to escape this foe? Where will I turn, where will I go?

Are there enough drugs to numb the pain,

or is drinking the vice that will work again?

"No!" my soul cries. "Pain will not win."

This time it won't take me back into sin—for there is a Savior who died for me.

And He conquered pain so I could be free.

He will give me the strength I need for today; He's what I need to take pain away.

"Jesus loves me. This I know, for the Bible tells me so. Little ones to Him belong; they are weak, but He is strong"! (Anna B. Warner; 1860)

Pain is a vicious thing, a black monster stalking its prey, watching and waiting for a moment to strike. Pain keeps pen from paper. It silences stories by making us feel like we will die if anyone finds out the truth about who we are and what we've done. It locks us in a world of fear and buries our emotions into a deep, dark hole in our heart. Pain makes us hide in fear of what exposure will do to us. It is cruel. It laughs and it jeers.

Yes, pain is a monster. A greedy monster that always wants more from you, more of your tears, more of your peace, more of your sanity. It cripples a person by taking his or her eyes off of the heavenly Father longing for you to have a "peace that passes understanding." (Phil. 4:7) KJV Pain brings shadows across your sunny world and darkens your blue-sky day. It creeps up on you and smothers your potential to grow into the person God created you to be. "In my anguish I cried to the Lord and He answered by setting me free" (Psalm 118:5). NIV

The enemy, Satan, uses pain to cripple us emotionally. He knows that if we deal with the pain, our stories can be used by God to set others free from their personal pain. Our story can help to heal another hurting person.

Dealing with pain is hard work. It's much easier to numb it—self-medicate with drugs—whether by a prescription or not. I've done both in the past. Before I reconciled my heart with God, I used a lot of illegal drugs to numb the pain. Then, after I surrendered my heart to the Lord, I knew that I couldn't use the old ways to curb the pain, so I went to the doctor and got prescription pills. I used over-the-counter medications too. Sometimes it's easier to just take a sleeping pill and forget it all. But I realized that living in the fog and haze of drugs prolongs the process of working through the pain. I had to give it totally to God, and one day at a time, He is bringing me through to a place where pain can no longer bully me and defeat me.

Pain tells us to be quiet but God says He can use us. We are meant for more than we can imagine. Yes, yes, we are! Pain keeps us from sharing our hard, ugly stories, but those stories can be a lifeline to a drowning person.

I love the author Ann Voskamp. Her story, written in *One Thousand Gifts*, has encouraged me to grab hold of hope, to trust God with the hurt, and to let Him use my story to help someone who is in emotional need too.

September 11, 2001 Paints a Picture

Do you remember where you were on September 11, 2001? Do you remember the horror you felt as you watched the Twin Towers being destroyed? Didn't you feel helpless to stop the dust cloud of ashes and debris that rolled over the streets of New York City and covered everything and everyone in its path that day? Prior to 9/11, I had no words or pictures to describe what the abortion did to me, but as I stood in my living room that morning, watching the terrorism unfold on my television, it came to me. *What a bomb does to a building is what abortion does to a soul!* The horror of it may be buried for months—even years—but the very act of abortion creates a dust-cloud effect that seeps through every bone in your body until it threatens to suffocate the life out of you.

I have a close friend who lost her little boy when he was only two years old. Several months after Andrew died, his mother said to me that going through that experience was like "trying to live while holding your breath." That is how I felt for many, many years. There was no way possible for me to live life to its fullest while holding my breath.

Satan is a terrorist and he has used some of his biggest weapons against me. I have battled thoughts of suicide, drugs, and alcohol as well as many fears since my abortion. By God's grace I later met and married a caring and compassionate man, Keith, who loved me, scars and all. Sadly, he has taken the brunt of much of the trauma caused by my abortion, but to his credit, he has stood by me every step of the way.

It takes time to rebuild—whether it's a memorial like the one in New York City for victims of 9/11—or a soul like mine. Satan wanted me destroyed, but you know what? God says, in Isaiah 61:3, that He will give joy for mourning, praise for a spirit of heaviness, and best of all, beauty for ashes! Even the ashes of abortion!

> The spirit of the Lord God is upon me, because the Lord has anointed me to preach good tidings to the poor; He has sent me to heal the brokenhearted, to proclaim liberty to the captives and the opening of the prison to those who are bound; to proclaim the acceptable year of the Lord and the day of vengeance of our God; to COMFORT all who mourn, to console those who mourn in Zion, to give them beauty for ashes. (Isaiah 61:1-3)

Ashes

For many years after my abortion I lived my life surrounded by a pile of ashes. My choice had burned a hole in my heart, and I was left to sift through the ashes every day. Do you know what happens when you hold ashes in your hands? That's right. You get dirty. When you are holding ashes in your hands, everything you touch gets dirty, too. Physically, spiritually, and mentally, I was streaked with ashes of regret, bitterness, and anger. I could sift through them every day if I wanted. I could stay covered from head to toe in them. Most of my struggle, even to this day, comes from wanting to sift through the ashes of regret. I just want to hold May 9, 1984, in my hands and rub them together until they are so black, they won't ever come clean.

Some days I don't feel like I deserve to be clean. I did this terrible thing and Satan wants me to stay dirty for the rest of my life. He wants me to believe that God sees me covered in ashes. This is how Satan kept me from fighting in the battle raging in the world today about abortion. He wants me to roll in the black ashes and throw a pity party. But if I do then how will the world know what the ramifications of abortion are? How will the next generation be able to make better choices if I don't speak up and out?

These days, when I want to sift through the ashes of regret, I turn to Isaiah. He didn't have to have an abortion to know that we are all unclean before God. Listen to what Isaiah says in chapter 1:16. "O wash yourselves! Be clean! Let me no longer see you doing all these wicked things."

I especially love Isaiah 1:18.

> "Come, let us talk this over!" says the Lord; "No matter how deep the stain of your sins, I can take it out and make you as clean as freshly fallen snow. Even if you are stained as red as crimson, I can make you white as wool."

My heart cries out, *Yes! Yes! I want to be clean. Wash all of me, Lord, and use the ashes of my regret to help others know that they too can be clean.* Bitterness and anger can be washed away if you want them to be. Take them to God, and leave them at the foot of the cross forever. Never pick up those ashes again. Let God's love for you wash you from head to toe through the precious blood of our Savior, Jesus Christ. He is our advocate. He is the one who stands before God daily and cries, "She is clean!" Thank you, Jesus!

Mother's Day

Have you had an abortion? Or do you know someone who has? If so, maybe you have been suffering every Mother's Day in a church somewhere, just like I did, wishing you could do it over and have all of your children with you. Or you might be wishing you had the guts to drive your car off the road and end it all to see if God will let you into heaven so you can see the child you didn't keep.

I know. I've been there. Guilt will drive you to the edge of insanity, and if you don't find comfort in God's word, guilt can push you over the edge. David says in Psalm 51:14, "Deliver me from the guilt of bloodshed, O God, The God of my salvation, and my tongue shall sing aloud of Your righteousness."

Most every year, as Mother's Day weekend drew near, I struggled with how to enjoy it. Some years I asked my husband to take our family on a camping trip so I could get away from the crowd at church and the noisy restaurants with crying babies who were tired and hungry after being in church nurseries all morning.

Growing up in a Christian home meant going to church all dressed up with a corsage on your dress or lapel in honour or memory of your mother. Happy, excited mothers strolled into church on Mother's Day. It was their moment in the spotlight for all the hard work and time they put into their family during the year.

The congregations that I grew up in loved to give their mothers each a gift before the service started. There was a gift for the oldest mother, a gift for the youngest mother, a gift for the mother with the most children, etc. There were lots and lots of gifts for just a select few. Depending on the size of the congregation, this could go on for what seemed like an eternity to someone, me, sitting there with a guilty conscience. I didn't feel like I deserved to be acknowledged on Mother's Day, let alone enjoy any of it.

I realize now that this is a lie from Satan. It is his goal to keep us in bondage and shame. He wants God's children to be miserable. I began to compose a poem, adding one line on each Mother's Day, to try to aleviate my sorrow. Only after being healed in 2011 did I add the last few lines.

Mother's Day

There's another kind of mother in the church on Mother's Day.

She sits there, quietly watching, as you bow your head to pray.

She knows that you would judge her if she ever told the truth,

But God cries, "She's forgiven—the cross is all the proof."

She whispers softly in her heart,

Dear Lord, I am so sorry for this thing that I have done. As my children gather 'round me,

You know I'm missing one.

Her heart is full of sorrow; her mind is full of grief—how innocence was lost in a time of unbelief.

Precious child up there in heaven, how she wishes you were here.

If only she had wanted you on Mother's Day that year.

The music starts. The speaker speaks. She brushes back a tear.

She holds her secret tightly

'cause she knows just what you'd say

if you knew the truth about her this year on Mother's Day.

But if you are that girl or lady or friend. This isn't the way it has to end.

For those who know God's saving grace will never deny you a warm embrace.

Just keep your eyes upon the cross, and let the Redeemer redeem your loss.

Baby Girl or Baby Boy?

For anyone who has had an abortion, I pray that she will find healing and maybe, one day, come to pray and ask God to reveal the sex of her baby, like I did.

In order to survive, I locked any thoughts of my abortion in a room in my heart. Occasionally, through the years, I would crack the door open a bit, only to slam it shut. I just wasn't sure I could go there. I couldn't forget it either. I started reading a book called *Her Choice to Heal* by Sydna Massey and Joan Phillips. I read the book in bits and pieces. It was hard work, but I got through it. In it, the authors suggested I should ask God to tell me if that room in my heart was painted pink or blue. He revealed to me that it was pink—a baby girl! Then I prayed and asked God to help me name her. My precious baby's name is Alexis Grace. I call her Lexigrace.

When reading *Her Choice to Heal*, I found out about the National Memorial for the Unborn. It is located in Chattanooga, Tennessee. You can order a plaque with your child's name on it. They will send you one, and if you can't go there, they will mount one on the memorial wall for you. You can go to their website and look up your plaque and see your memorial to your child any time, day or night. This is a tremendous source of comfort for me.

The Book of Esther

Beth Moore has been my spiritual hero for many years now. God has used her Bible studies to help me grow and get to a place where I could confront the sordid past. One in particular, *Esther*, made me realize that I needed to finally confide in someone other than my husband.

In 2009, I began to feel that God wanted me to share my story with my Bible study leader, Cindy, who also happened to be my best friend. She was the girlfriend with whom I had shared the last fifteen years or more of my life. We had raised our kids together, gone on many vacations together, and attended the same church. We had shared personal issues with each other, but this one thing I had never told her about. I was very afraid of losing her friendship, but God would not give me peace until I told her.

Looking back, I wish I had done it differently because I chose to do it in a very public place—a shopping mall! I don't know why I picked such a place. Maybe it was so that I wouldn't break down and cry, but I did tell her, and it was a turning point for me. She was sad but so very supportive. She bravely shouldered this burden with me.

I have her to thank, too, for where I am today. She obeyed God when He called her into the ladies' ministry at our church to begin leading the Bible studies. The one we had just finished was Beth Moore's study on the book of Esther. Through it I began to hear God speak to me about who I was. I was a post-abortive woman, and I had a people, just like Esther did. God asked Esther to remember who she was and decide if she would help her people or not. Thank goodness she chose to let God use her. By doing the book of Esther Bible study, I realized that I needed to choose to be brave and share my story too. I had to believe God would protect me from the enemy. Just like Esther, I had to be truthful because my people, who are post-abortive women, matter to me. Finally, through my Bible study on Esther, God brought me to the realization that Satan wanted me destroyed, just like he wanted Esther and her people destroyed. John 10:10 says that "Satan comes to steal, kill and destroy."

> These angels unawares fighting battles I can't see these angels unawares holding back the enemy God grant them strength to war and win give them the power to help me again. These angels unawares fighting battles I can't see- they give me hope, protection and a mighty victory! *–agg*

I had to come to the conclusion that, in order to help other women and girls, I had to tell the truth about my past. Over the years, Satan has tried to destroy me but he didn't get his way. Praise be to God who has saved me and brought me to this place in my life!

After sharing my past with Cindy, I waited and waited for two years before God led me to the next step in my healing process. I guess I was still too scared to go forward because I struggled with such guilt. Like I said in the beginning, telling someone doesn't fix the facts, and I was still an emotional wreck. I knew that God loved me, but I couldn't get the forgiveness part in my head or my heart. I still let Satan use false guilt to beat me up on a daily basis. It was a miserable two years!

Surrendering the Secret

While reading a monthly devotional one day in January 2011, I was introduced to Pat Layton. Pat is a wonderful lady who has been in ministry for more than twenty-five years. She knows first-hand what it's like to live with the guilt of an abortion and with the relief of God's saving grace and forgiveness.

For many years she has run a pregnancy crisis center in Tampa, Florida. She teaches a ladies' conference called "Imagine Me Set Free."

She has also written a wonderful Bible study for post-abortive women called "Surrendering the Secret." It is put out by Lifeway and is an excellent resource for those who have had an abortion or know someone who has.

I ordered the set, leader's guide and all, and used it at home by myself. I couldn't have written this book without having first gone through that study. I am at a point in my life where I know that, in order to heal, I have to be willing to "surrender the secret." I want to be free to share where I've come from and how I got to where I am today. I want to stand before God empty, not empty-handed. I have a story to pour out, to empty from my heart before it's too late.

Completing the Bible study in my home was the start of my journey to find someone whom I could sit down with personally. I needed to have a real hand to hold, a real person to help wipe away my tears. I prayed for God to lead me to such a person, and in the fall of that year, He did. Through various circumstances, He connected me with a counselor at the Refuge Pregnancy center in my hometown. They offered a seven week program called H.E.A.R.T. (Healing the Effects of Abortion Related Trauma) I signed up for it and continued to "surrender my secret."

Comfort

I have several very close friends in whom I have confided. They are well acquainted with grief because they have lost close family members throughout the years. One of the most precious memories I have is of them comforting me on a Sunday night after a church service. We had a special concert that night, and I was caught off guard by the closing song about abortion.

I was so grateful for the hugs of reassurance from them that night, and I'm just as thankful now. I didn't receive comfort the day I walked out of the abortion clinic. I wasn't allowed to grieve. It's tragic, but true—society turns on post-abortive women by pointing a finger and saying, "It was your choice, therefore you don't deserve to grieve." In order to be healed we have to grieve because repressed grief can cause all kinds of problems both physically and mentally. "Blessed are they that mourn for they shall be comforted" (Matthew 5:4). KJV

If you have had an abortion, please know that you too can be comforted. God is a God of mercy and grace! Ask Him to reveal a special person in whom you can confide in. Pray for someone who will let you cry on his or her shoulder and hold you when you need to be held.

You deserve to grieve, and you deserve to be comforted. "Blessed be God . . . the God of all comfort who comforts us in all our tribulation so that we may be able to comfort those who mourn" (II Corinthians 1:3-4). KJV

Refuge Crisis Pregnancy Center

At the end of 2011, God had worked a tremendous miracle in my life. From January to December 2011, through various programs, He had orchestrated events that brought me to a place of great healing. The one that helped me to heal the most was working through a program called H.E.A.R.T.—a one-on-one, seven-week Bible study facilitated by a counselor at my local pregnancy center. From day one, I was a bundle of emotions. Tears fell uninhibited because I was finally in the presence of someone who knew how I felt and who had walked the valleys I had walked. I didn't know it then, but she would be beside me as I began to climb the mountain path that God was leading me toward in 2012.

Her name is Angela, and she is the most precious person in the world to me now. She held my hand and cried with me, just like I was the only person she had ever helped through PAS, even though she has been facilitating this program for more than seven years now. I can't even begin to thank her. I know she wouldn't accept the praise anyway; she would just look me in the eye and assure me that our God gets all the praise. And He does. Thank you, heavenly Father.

I believe that our faith and actions work together. As James 2:22 notes, our faith is made complete by what we do for the Lord. One day at a time, God has sustained me and brought me to this season in my life so that I can help others by volunteering at Refuge Pregnancy center myself.

> They that sow in tears will reap with songs of joy. He who goes out weeping, carrying seed to sow, will return with songs of joy, carrying sheaves with him. (Psalm 126:5, 6)NIV

Lexigrace

After I completed the H.E.A.R.T. program at my local pregnancy crisis center, my counselor, Angela, arranged for a pastor to hold a private baby dedication service for my daughter, Lexigrace, and me.

The day will stay in my mind forever. My counselor, the pastor, and I met in a little chapel in my hometown. We pulled our chairs into a circle and held hands as the pastor prayed. Then he shared out of the Bible, from 1 Samuel 21, what God had laid on his heart.

The bible tells how David had made friends with the enemy, Saul, and that, as a result, David had gone into hiding. He began running for his life and lying because his enemy wanted him dead. Many innocent people were killed because of David, but *God had other plans for David's life. He wanted David to be king!*

I realized that I too had made friends with the enemy and was in hiding. For many years, I had been running for my life, lying and living in fear. An innocent life had been taken.

The enemy wanted me dead, but *God had other plans for my life. He wanted me redeemed—He wanted to make me a queen!* So He pursued me, and He took back the years that the enemy had stolen. He restored my soul!

On February 9, 2012, my life was placed back on the path that God had ordained for me.

The pastor signed a certificate of dedication for Lexigrace and for me. I will cherish it forever. One of the last exercises in the H.E.A.R.T. program was for me to write a letter to Lexigrace and bring it to the dedication to read out loud to her.

I will share part of it with you.

> Alexis Grace,
> I am here today in honour of your memory. Although your life on this earth was brief, it was real. For just a few weeks, many years ago, you were a part of me physically, and I want you to know that I remember.
> I also want you to know that I will never again forget. From the edges of heaven I can hear your sweet voice whispering, "I love you, Mommy."
> With tears of joy, I will say your name out loud whenever I need to, and one day, Lexigrace, we will be together in heaven. I cannot wait to see you and hold you for the first time. What a day that will be, precious girl!"

After reading my letter, the three of us walked outside, and I released a pink balloon. With bittersweet tears, I watched as it floated out of sight, all the while thinking of this verse

> There is now no condemnation awaiting those who belong to Jesus Christ. For the power of the

life-giving Spirit—and this power is mine through Christ Jesus has freed me from the vicious circle of sin and death. (Romans 8:1, 2 TLB)

Thank you, Jesus!

I am so thankful that God led me to Refuge and Angela. I accomplished a great deal by doing the homework in the H.E.A.R.T. program. Letters were written and read out loud, not to be sent but to help with the healing process. I later burned a few of them—more "beauty from ashes."

Several I kept and will always treasure though. One was a letter I had to write from Lexigrace to me. I remember sitting at my kitchen table and asking God to speak to me and tell me what my daughter would want me to hear. What would she have to say to me? This is what my pen put to paper.

> Dear Mom,
> Do you know how happy I am? All I ever wanted was for you to know that I am alive and well. I wanted you to know that I exist; I am real. I know you know that now, and I will spend every day in heaven telling everyone about you. I will tell them how special my mom is because she did what it took to come to a place of healing so that she could help others. I will tell them that you are my best friend and the most wonderful mom a girl could ever have. Don't you worry, Mom, I forgive you. I forgave you a long time ago because Jesus

helped me to understand it all, right from the start. We both love you so much! That's all I ever wanted—to have you know that I love you and to have you love me back.

Love,
Lexigrace

December 2011
P.S. Merry Christmas!

So there it is. My love letter from my precious daughter whom I have waiting on me in heaven.

One day I will walk out of this life on earth and enter my heavenly home. I will no longer be afraid of death or facing my heavenly Father. I have been forgiven of all the evil that my abortion set in motion, and I can look forward to walking the streets of gold in peace—no more worrying if God will let me in or about the reception I will face. I have a future that is bright with hope and anticipation. And when I die, I want to die empty of all the good works that God, my Father, has prepared for me to do in advance. I hope my life story helps others find release from the prison of their abortions. I want to shout from the rooftop that there is freedom for the captives who still live with the torment that only an enemy of God would put on them for having had an abortion. And most of all, I want my life to be a work of beauty, beauty from ashes (Isaiah 61:3). "The Spirit and the bride say, 'Come!' and let him who hears say, 'Come!' Whoever is thirsty, let him come; and whoever wishes, let him take the free gift of the water of life" (Revelations 22:17).

I cannot wait for God to reunite me with my daughter in heaven one day!

"He who testifies to these things says, 'Yes, I am coming quickly.' Amen. Come, Lord Jesus" (Revelations 22:20).

December 30, 2011

Healing from an abortion is a process. When you grieve for someone, you never get over it; you just get through it one day at a time. The enemy of this world knows that abortion is one of the most powerful tools he can use against us because it has the power to cripple and silence us.

As I sit at the kitchen table, my thoughts turn back to the past year. In my healing journey, I don't know how many miles I've covered with God this year, but I know it has been many. From the article written by Pat Layton in *Journey* magazine, Beth Moore bible studies, all the way to the H.E.A.R.T. program that I completed with a counselor, God has walked with me. I have searched for my place to minister to girls in crisis. I've participated in *40 Days For Life* by standing vigil and praying for those entering a local abortion clinic. My heart broke for the girls I saw going into the clinic. I had been in their shoes. I knew they thought they were fixing their problem, but in reality, they weren't. They just didn't know it yet. For some, the realization may never come, but for others—maybe the next day, maybe twenty years down the road—they will remember and weep over their decisions. I pray that they will find someone to lead them through a healing process that will gently restore their soul.

A Final Note

One of my very favorite verses in the Bible is John 21:25. "Jesus did many other things as well. If every one of them were written down, I suppose that even the whole world could not have room for the books that would be written."

What if each one of us wrote our own stories down? And what if we added the stories of what Jesus did in us as well? Do you think there would be enough room in this world for the books that would be written? I don't.

I know, too, that not everyone will be compelled to write their stories, but I was because "Deep calls to deep" (Psalm 42:7). I have been deeply hurt, and I have been deeply forgiven. Today I want to give back to those who are in deep distress over an unplanned pregnancy or an abortion experience. Twenty-five years ago, few women were willing to speak out about the trauma of having an abortion and post-abortion syndrome. There are more now, and I think that we need every story to be told. It's the only way for future generations of women and girls to know how terrible the choice of abortion can be.

My message is His message: I am forgiven. If it can help just one person, then it will be worth it all.

If you are reading this and have had an abortion, please feel free to contact me. I would love to let you know that someone else knows how you feel. Sometimes no words are necessary, but physical comfort, a look of understanding, or a gentle word of encouragement are all that's needed to get us through this life.

If you are one of my girlfriends with whom I timidly shared my story in the beginning of my healing process, then know this: I love you and thank you from the bottom of my heart for not turning away from me. Thank you for your support; I would not have made it without you or your hugs!

And last of all, if you are a family member, please know that I have prayed over whether to tell you my story or not. In my healing journey, I have learned that sometimes it's better not to tell. Philippians 4:8 tells us to think on things that are pure and lovely—my story is not pure and lovely, but it does have a happy ending! I know that God has a plan and purpose for me to fulfill on this earth. It has been my prayer for God to lead me each step of the way in all that I do or say. My goal is to help others, but not hurt anyone in the process. However, I realize that there may come a time that I have to make a choice to tell my story to help another person. I am willing to do that, and I pray that you will understand.

Bibliography

International Bible Society. *The Holy Bible, New International Version*. Grand Rapids: Zondervan, 2005.

Layton, Pat. *Surrendering the Secret*. Nashville: Lifeway Press, 2008.

Lucado, Max. *The Lucado Life Lessons Study Bible, New King James Version*. Nashville: Thomas Nelson, Inc., 2010.

Masse, Sydna, and Joan Phillips. *Her Choice to Heal*. Colorado Springs: Chariot Victor Publishing, 1998.

Masse, Sydna. *Her Choice to Heal*. Colorado Springs: Ramah International, 2001

Moore, Beth. *Esther: It's Tough Being a Woman*. Nashville: Lifeway Press, 2008.

—*James: Mercy Triumphs*. Nashville: Lifeway Press, 2011.

Tyndale. *The Living Bible*. Wheaton: Tyndale House Publishers,1973.

Voskamp, Ann. *One Thousand Gifts*. Grand Rapids: Zondervan, 2010.

Zodhiates, Spiros. *King James Version, Hebrew Greek Key Study Guide*. Chattanooga: AMG Publishers, 1998.

H.E.A.R.T. Manual.: Heartbeat International, Columbus, Ohio, 1993.

Printed in the United States
By Bookmasters